# Finding My Voice

*Youth with Speech Impairment*

# Finding My Voice

*Youth with Speech Impairment*

BY JOYCE LIBAL

MASON CREST PUBLISHERS

Mason Crest Publishers Inc.
370 Reed Road
Broomall, Pennsylvania 19008
(866) MCP-BOOK (toll free)

First printing
1 2 3 4 5 6 7 8 9 10

Libal, Joyce.
Finding my voice: youth with speech impairment / by Joyce Libal.
v. cm.—(Youth with special needs)
Includes bibliographical references and index.
Contents: The calm before the storm—From bad to worse—Cloistered in a world of voice—Envying Martha—Searching for self—A time for discoveries—A new day.
1. Speech disorders in children—Juvenile literature. 2. Language disorders in children—Juvenile literature. 3. Communicative disorders in children—Juvenile literature. 4. Speech therapy—Juvenile literature. [1. Speech disorders. 2. People with physical disabilities.] I. Title. II. Series.
RJ496.S7L53 2004
618.92'855—dc22.    2003018639
ISBN 1-59084-738-5
1-59084-727-X (series)


Design by Harding House Publishing Service.
Composition by Bytheway Publishing Services, Inc., Binghamton, New York.
Cover art by Keith Rosco.
Cover design by Benjamin Stewart.
Produced by Harding House Publishing Service, Vestal, New York.
Printed and bound in the Hashemite Kingdom of Jordan.

**Picture credits:** Artville: p. 120; Autumn Libal: pp. 16, 19; Benjamin Stewart: pp. 22, 35, 38, 39, 43, 45, 46, 53, 55, 56, 58, 67, 68, 69, 70, 71, 72, 88, 98, 99; Corel: p. 42; Dover, *Dictionary of American Portraits*: p. 101; Life Art: pp. 34, 37, 40; Photo Alto: pp. 31, 32, 36, 74, 102, 103, 115, 117, 118; PhotoDisc: pp. 15, 33, 41, 82, 83, 84, 87, 97, 104, 112, 113. Individuals in Corel, Photo Alto, and PhotoDisc images are models, and the images are intended for illustrative purposes only.

# CONTENTS

A child with special needs is not defined by his disability.
It is just one part of who he is.

# Introduction

Each child is unique and wonderful. And some children have differences we call special needs. Special needs can mean many things. Sometimes children will learn differently, or hear with an aid, or read with Braille. A young person may have a hard time communicating or paying attention. A child can be born with a special need, or acquire it by an accident or through a health condition. Sometimes a child will be developing in a typical manner and then become delayed in that development. But whatever problems a child may have with her learning, emotions, behavior, or physical body, she is always a person first. She is not defined by her disability; instead, the disability is just one part of who she is.

Inclusion means that young people with and without special needs are together in the same settings. They learn together in school; they play together in their communities; they all have the same opportunities to belong. Children learn so much from each other. A child with a hearing impairment, for example, can teach another child a new way to communicate using sign language. Someone else who has a physical disability affecting his legs can show his friends how to play wheelchair basketball. Children with and without special needs can teach each other how to appreciate and celebrate their differences. They can also help each other discover how people are more alike than they are different. Understanding and appreciating how we all have similar needs helps us learn empathy and sensitivity.

In this series, you will read about young people with special needs from the unique perspectives of children and adolescents who are experiencing the disability firsthand. Of course, not all children with a particular disability are the same as the characters in the stories. But the stories demonstrate at an emotional level how a special need impacts a child, his family, and his friends. The factual material in each chapter will expand your horizons by adding to your knowledge about a particular disability. The series as a whole will help you understand differences better and appreciate how they make us all stronger and better.

—*Cindy Croft*
*Educational Consultant*

YOUTH WITH SPECIAL NEEDS provides a unique forum for demystifying a wide variety of childhood medical and developmental disabilities. Written to captivate an adolescent audience, the books bring to life the challenges and triumphs experienced by children with common chronic conditions such as hearing loss, mental retardation, physical differences, and speech difficulties. The topics are addressed frankly through a blend of fiction and fact. Students and teachers alike can move beyond the information provided by accessing the resources offered at the end of each text.

This series is particularly important today as the number of children with special needs is on the rise. Over the last two decades, advances in pediatric medical techniques have allowed children who have chronic illnesses and disabilities to live longer, more functional lives. As a result, these children represent an increasingly visible part of North American population in all aspects of daily life. Students are exposed to peers with special needs in their classrooms, through extracurricular activities, and in the community. Often, young people have misperceptions and unanswered questions about a child's disabilities—and more important, his or her *abilities*. Many times, there is no vehicle for talking about these complex issues in a comfortable manner.

This series provides basic information that will leave readers with a deeper understanding of each condition, along with an awareness of some of the associated emotional impacts on affected children, their families, and their peers. It will also encourage further conversation about these issues. Most important, the series promotes a greater comfort for its readers as they live, play, and work side by side with these individuals who have medical and developmental differences—youth with special needs.

*—Dr. Lisa Albers, Dr. Carolyn Bridgemohan, Dr. Laurie Glader*
*Medical Consultants*

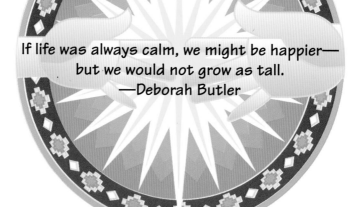

If life was always calm, we might be happier—
but we would not grow as tall.
—Deborah Butler

# 1

# THE CALM BEFORE
# THE STORM

The Miller baby must have been anxious to be born, for he did so quickly and easily. Leon held Ellie's hand as he watched his son's birth. "He has all his fingers and toes; he's perfect, Ellie," Leon announced proudly. The nurse-midwife handed the baby to his mother, who smiled with satisfaction, relief, and joy while caressing her new baby. It was love at first sight for both parents, just as it had been when their other children were born.

David Miller entered the world as all babies do, completely innocent and helpless, and without a language to frame his thoughts. Light, dark, heat, cold, hunger, satisfaction, discomfort, and care were felt from the beginning, but he had no frame of reference in which to place these feelings, and he lacked a way of expressing them or communicating his exact needs to others.

It became immediately clear, however, that David had a healthy set of lungs and vocal cords; he displayed his voice to his parents when he cried for the first time. Reacting with well-practiced instinct, Leon and Ellie immediately responded to their son's call. "What's the matter, little guy? Are you hungry already?" Leon asked softly as Ellie placed her son to her breast.

A few hours later, David's siblings visited him for the first time. "Can we hold him?" Karen asked.

Leon carefully lifted his new son from Ellie's arms and showed Karen how to gently cradle him in hers.

Theresa became impatient as Leon next transferred the baby to Lily and then to Leon Jr. "Isn't it my tawn yet?" she pleaded.

"Yes, it's your turn, Theresa," her father replied, placing the baby in her arms.

"I still think we should call him Twevah," Theresa said, wishing that everyone would agree to her favorite name.

"Theresa!" Leon Jr. said in an exasperated tone, "we've been through this a million times. Everybody else wants to call him David. I don't understand why you want to call him a name you can't even pronounce!"

"I'm lawning to talk betta," Theresa said in defense of herself, but some of the joy went out of the day for her when attention was placed on her speech impairment. She looked past the baby and down to the floor as she began to cry.

"Leon Jr!" his mother admonished, "you know better than that. Your sister is working hard with the speech therapist at school, and soon she'll be pronouncing her R's beautifully. I can already notice lots of improvement."

"Weally?" Theresa asked hopefully, glancing up at her mother.

"Yes, really," Ellie responded. "I have an idea. We haven't picked out a middle name for the baby yet. Why don't we call him David Trevor Miller?"

"That sounds great to me," Leon responded. "What do you kids think?"

Theresa beamed with happiness. "I like David Twevah Millah."

"Me too," Karen and Lily said in unison, and even Leon Jr. agreed.

David Trevor Miller was soon the center of attention in the Miller household. Gradually the bright-eyed newborn became alert to the activity that was taking place around him. He was the delight of his brother and sisters as he began to smile and wiggle with excitement when they talked to him or held his chubby hands.

The older Miller children were unaware of all the language instruction they were providing to their brother. Like all babies his age, David was busy gaining information about the world. All his gurgling and babbling was his way of learning how to manipulate sound.

When David was six months old, Ellie decided to return to work half days. The triplets were now in first grade and Leon Jr. was in sixth, his final year at the elementary school. Since Ellie and Leon both went to work each weekday morning, David began to spend his mornings with several other babies and toddlers in a day-care center. After a rough couple of days, he adjusted well to his new caregivers. Ellie picked him up at about 1:00 P.M. each weekday and was glad to see that he retained his happy demeanor. The pediatrician was satisfied that David's height and weight; all aspects of his development were on track.

By the time he was a year old, David was beginning to say his first words—*Mama* and *Dada*. Shortened versions of his brother's and sisters' names came next, followed by *wawa* for water and *mmmm* for everything that tasted good. Language was developing very quickly for David, and with each week that passed, his understanding and vocabulary grew.

Ellie and Leon were happy, too, that Theresa had made great strides with the speech therapist. They had been concerned that David might pick up Theresa's mispronunciation of the R sound, but that didn't happen. By the second grade, Theresa's pronunciation was perfect, and she graduated out of speech therapy.

With five active children and both parents employed, the Miller household seemed busier than ever. Yet, in later years, Ellie would come to look back on these days as a peaceful and carefree time. Big challenges were about to enter her family's life.

It began innocently on the morning of the triplets' ninth birthday. David was three and a half years old and had spent the previous afternoon helping his mother decorate three small cakes. When Ellie woke him that morning for day care, the first thing out of his mouth was, "Wh-wh-where are the cakes?" Ellie never gave the repeated syllables a second thought as she whispered an answer.

"Remember that the cakes are a secret, David. The school bus hasn't come yet, and your sisters are still in the kitchen. I hid the cakes in the cupboard. We'll surprise the girls with them after supper tonight. Until then, don't say anything to anybody about them. Understand?"

"Ooooookkkay," David replied.

# THE MAGIC OF SPEECH— HOW DOES IT HAPPEN?

People use many different nonverbal signals when communicating with each other. We shake hands when introduced to someone for the first time as a way of saying that we're pleased to meet the person. A hug can be a gesture of friendship or love. A smile tells others that we are happy and a frown indicates displeasure. Our foreheads wrinkle sometimes when we are puzzled, and our eyebrows arch when we are surprised. Of all the different ways that people communicate, however, speech is the major tool that we use for sharing information. It is one of the most important components of civilization and of individual cultures. Speech is also the basis for written language.

Speech happens quickly, yet it is actually quite complicated. Although you don't have to think about it consciously while talking, as you pronounce individual words and form sentences many different body parts must move in a precise

*Our facial expressions and the positions of our bodies communicate our emotions to others.*

and coordinated way in order to make the needed sounds. It all begins with the brain and breath. We decide to speak and inhale. When we do this, our **vocal folds** (two smooth bands of muscular tissue that are positioned opposite each other) come together. As we begin to exhale, the air vibrates the vocal folds, which makes sound. Hold your breath and try to speak. Were you successful? More likely, you discovered that without breath it is impossible to speak.

By changing the amount of air we inhale, the way we exhale, and the way we move the parts of our mouth as our voice passes through it, we can change the way that we speak. To gain a better understanding of this, compare it to blowing up a balloon and then releasing the air. As you hold the valve of the balloon, you can control the amount of air being released. You can alter the sound somewhat by pulling the valve tighter or making it looser.

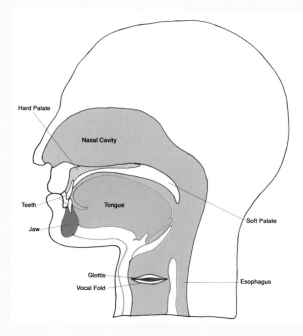

When we are not speaking, our vocal folds remain open so that we can breathe. The exact shape and size of your vocal folds, mouth, throat, and nose all play a part in the distinct sound of your voice.

## Many Parts of the Body Are Used When Making Speech

- brain
- lungs
- nose
- lips
- tongue
- teeth
- jaws
- throat (the throat cavity is called the pharynx)
- velum (soft palate)
- hard palate
- larynx, also called the voice box (The true vocal folds, which are also called the vocal cords, and the glottis, which is the opening between the vocal folds, are located here.)
- trachea, also called the windpipe (This is the air passage to the lungs.)
- other muscles in your mouth

By manipulating parts of the mouth and using the other body parts listed above, we produce speech. Make the sounds listed below aloud while paying attention to the parts of your body that are used to produce them.

- Make the M sound. Now hold your nose closed and make the M sound.
- Make the B sound. Now make the B sound without moving your lips.

- Make the T sound. Now make the T sound while keeping your tongue at the bottom of your mouth.

Practice making more individual speech sounds while paying attention to the parts of the body that you use and the position that you place them in. You'll notice that to make specific sounds, various body parts must be placed in the correct position. Sometimes people have difficulty achieving the correct placement to make each sound.

Say the following words aloud. Speak slowly and think about the different body parts you are using as you make all the sound combinations that are necessary for these words:

- antelope
- monochromatic
- caricature
- diplomacy
- chisel
- thalamus
- pictorial
- ingredients
- zipper
- Mississippi

## SPEECH IMPAIRMENT

When someone has a **speech impairment**, it is more difficult for him to use his body parts correctly or quickly enough to make the sounds and movements necessary for speech than it is for the average person to do so. Imagine how hard it would be to say the words we listed above if you had difficulty moving and controlling the parts of your mouth that are necessary to talk.

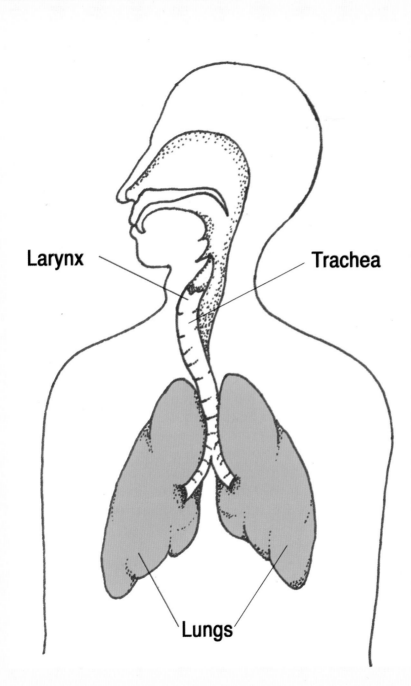

Larynx

Trachea

Lungs

# HOW IS LANGUAGE LEARNED?

We begin to learn to understand language and to speak from our parents, other caregivers, and siblings when we are babies. The acquisition of language usually happens informally and without special training, but it is affected by *cognitive* ability and by the type of exposure to language that babies receive. Each person is an individual, and each environmental and family situation is unique; some of us begin speaking extremely early, while others take a much longer time to learn to talk. Most babies begin purposeful babbling at about six months of age and speak their first words at about twelve months. Some sounds that are necessary for speech are learned later than others. Between the ages of two and four years old, most children are in a vigorous stage of language development.

# WATCHING BABY

When a baby's speech development is noticeably slower than what has come to be expected of babies the same age, it is considered to be delayed. Researchers have determined that it is easiest to learn speech and language skills as the brain is developing prior to the age of five. Hearing is essential to the acquisition of speech and language skills, so any hearing loss can cause delayed development. Because the acquisition of speech is extremely important to all other learning and social skills, it is important to identify and treat developmental delays as early as possible, before they become disorders that have a negative impact on other learning. The chart on the next page displays the ages by which most babies and young children have demonstrated the listed abilities. Babies who have not reached these developmental goals should be tested for proper hearing levels.

| | |
|---|---|
| Young infants | From birth to approximately three months old, babies should demonstrate that they are startled by unexpected sounds. Additionally, their behavior should begin to demonstrate that they are comforted by the sound of their parents' or caretakers' voices. |
| By six months | Babies should show that they are interested in noisy toys such as rattles, and they should turn their head and eyes toward various sounds. |
| By ten months | Babies should understand simple words like yes and no, mommy and daddy, peek-a-boo and bye-bye, and they should react to their names. They should also demonstrate a reaction to sounds like the telephone ringing or a dog barking, even if they cannot see the source of the sound. |
| By fifteen months | Babies should demonstrate that they understand many words; for example, they should be able to point to an appropriate object when asked to do so. Additionally, they should be imitating speech sounds. |
| By eighteen months | Babies this age should be saying a few simple words, be able to recognize many objects (such as dog, house, car, etc.), and be able to follow simple directions. |
| By two years old | These children should be speaking simple phrases and should understand yes/no questions. |
| By thirty months | The vocabulary of a child this age should have grown to encompass more than 250 words. |
| By three years old | The vocabulary of a child this age should have grown to encompass approximately 1,000 words. These children should be speaking in complete sentences that include simple verbs, adjectives, and pronouns. |
| By four years old | Children should be able to follow simple directions that involve two steps and be able to talk about an event they experienced. |
| By five years old | When these children speak, they should be easily understood by people who are not related to them. |

*Babies learn to speak as they play.*

The vast majority of people are not perfect at any given task the first time that they try it. It takes time and patience to learn most skills, and speech is no exception. When children are learning how to speak, they usually make common errors in phonology such as leaving the ending sounds off of words or replacing a sound that is difficult to make with one that sounds similar but is made more easily (substituting the T sound for the K sound, for example). Most of these mispronunciations are outgrown as language develops. When they are not outgrown, however, they can cause learning difficulties or social problems with peers. If a child has reached the age of four and is still making these or other errors while speaking, it is a good idea to have the child's speech evaluated by a qualified professional. If a five-year-old child's speech cannot be understood by an adult who is not a family member, the child should definitely be evaluated by a speech pathologist or a speech therapist.

Emerson said, "Every wall is a door." When you're against the wall, remember—that's where you'll find the way out.
—Paula Burke

# 2

# FROM BAD TO WORSE

David didn't experience any more *disfluencies* that day, but over the next several weeks Ellie noticed a few occasions when David repeated or prolonged some of the sounds in words as he said them. Each time she told herself he was just tired. *After all, doesn't it usually happen in the morning when I wake him for day care or in the afternoon when he gets up from his nap?* she asked herself. *No one else has mentioned it. I don't think he's doing it all that much. It doesn't seem to bother him. I'm sure it's just a phase and nothing to worry about*, she tried to convince herself.

In truth, however, worry had already begun to eat at Ellie's heart. She loved her children, and each of them was perfect in her eyes. She had hopes and dreams for all of them, and none of her dreams included a health problem or other impairment. Each time David faltered as he spoke, Ellie grew more nervous about the situation. Still, she said nothing about it, even to Leon. She felt as though talking about it would make it worse somehow, would make it *real*. And she didn't want that. She wanted this thing, whatever it was, to go away, like a bad dream, and never return.

As David neared his fourth birthday, he was experiencing disfluencies on a regular basis, and everyone in the household had witnessed them. Leon was the one to first mention the subject. "Ellie, I'm concerned about David's speech," he began one evening.

"What do you mean?" Ellie responded innocently while thinking that she sounded like an idiot, because she knew full well what

**25**

her husband meant. *Why am I acting like I don't know what he's talking about?* she asked herself. *What's wrong with me? Why can't I say what I really think?*"

"I think you do know what I mean," Leon said, putting his arms around his wife to comfort her. "I think we need to get some help for David."

"Can't we wait just a little while?" his wife pleaded. "I think he's going through a phase. Remember when Leon Jr. started stuttering? He was about three, and it didn't last long at all. It stopped just as fast as it started. Maybe David is going to grow out of this soon."

Leon sighed. "Sure, we can wait a little while. Maybe it's normal and he'll grow out of it," he agreed hopefully.

The day-care workers were also worried, however, and they requested a conference with Ellie and Leon a couple of weeks later. "I'm sure you've noticed the change in David's speech," Ms. Wheeler began. "Ms. Taylor and I have become increasingly concerned about it."

"We think that David could benefit from an evaluation by a qualified speech pathologist," Ms. Taylor put in. "We're recommending an assessment by Harold Bennet. He's worked with several of the children here."

"Thank you." Leon was surprised to hear his wife answer so quickly. "We'll certainly take your suggestion under consideration. Will you please write down Mr. Bennet's number for us?" she continued. "We don't really have time to discuss this with you further today, but Leon and I will talk about all our options and make a decision that's in David's best interest."

Leon realized his wife was dismissing Ms. Wheeler and Ms. Taylor. He was surprised by her defensive reaction, but he decided to agree with her and discuss everything further when they were alone.

"I've been thinking," Ellie began when they got to the car. "I'm going to take a leave of absence from work. I really regret having put David in day care now. Maybe if I had stayed home with him, this never would have happened. Maybe being away from his family has upset him, and that's what brought on the stuttering."

Leon shook his head. "Ellie, don't go there. I'm sure none of this has anything to do with you working. David has always been a well-adjusted little boy. He loves his family, and he enjoys day care."

"Well, I'm still going to take a leave of absence from work. School will be out for the summer soon, and it will be good for all of the kids. I'm going to stay home, and I'm going to spend time trying to help our son get over this."

Leon hesitated and then said, "That's fine, but I think we can also help him by getting an evaluation from a speech pathologist as Ms. Wheeler and Ms. Taylor suggested. It can't hurt anything, Ellie. Letting an expert talk to David certainly isn't going to make him worse, and the pathologist might have some suggestions that could help a lot. Maybe he'll teach us some exercises that we can do with David over the summer. I'd like to see David make some significant progress before he enters preschool in the fall, and I know you would, too. What do you say?"

"I guess you're right; speech therapy certainly helped Theresa. I'll call for the appointment tomorrow," Ellie agreed. "You know, Leon, there's something else I've been thinking about doing for some time now. I bet we can find a lot of information about stuttering on the Internet. I've thought about going on-line a dozen times to research the topic, but each time I changed my mind. I just haven't been able to get myself to turn the computer on and take that the next step. I guess I've been afraid of what I might find out."

"I'm scared, too, Ellie. I want a perfect life for David. But we're not going to be able to help him achieve that by giving in to our fears and avoiding this problem. Let's be brave and work together to help our son."

Ellie gave Leon's hand a squeeze, "I know you're right. I'm so glad we're in this together. Let's check out stuttering on the Internet later tonight."

By the time the evening was over, Ellie and Leon had visited a half dozen Internet sites. What they read convinced them that while some disfluencies are perfectly normal, David's speech impairment was not going to disappear on its own. Their son needed to begin speech therapy immediately.

Mr. Bennet's evaluation a week later confirmed their findings.

As part of the evaluation, Mr. Bennet interviewed Ellie and Leon. He wanted to know as much as possible about David's environment, and he had some suggestions for the Millers about how to help David. "You know the pace of life in our modern society is so fast; many families are engaged in numerous activities. I don't know all the things that you and your children are involved in, and I'm not saying that you should cut back on any of it. But we do find that it often helps children like David if the family slows down the pace of their life."

Leon nodded. "We've already read that suggestion on the Internet, and we've been thinking of things that we can do to make our family life simpler and more relaxed."

"That's great," Mr. Bennet responded. "Some of the other things that we suggest are to model slow speech to David, the way that I'm speaking to you now. It shouldn't sound unnatural, just slower and more relaxed than most of us commonly talk. I'd also suggest that you caution your other children not to rush David when he speaks, avoid telling him to slow down, and don't be tempted to finish his sentences for him. I know you've said that you spend time reading to David every day. That's wonderful, and you should definitely continue that, but I'd also like to show you some ways to play with David that will help him practice his speech."

Ellie and Leon felt that Mr. Bennet's advice would be good for any child, and they put all of it into action as soon as they returned home. Additionally, David began to visit Mr. Bennet for therapy every week.

The family was ***diligent*** in their care of David, but despite their hard work, David did not improve. Both Ellie and Leon hid their disappointment and continued working with their son on his speech patterns as instructed. As David's fifth birthday approached, however, Ellie confessed her worries to Leon.

"I thought by this time we'd see *something* encouraging."

"I know, but let's hang in there. At least David's speech hasn't deteriorated. If we hadn't started him in therapy, maybe it would have gotten worse. Why don't we concentrate on the fact that he has a big birthday coming up. What should we do to celebrate?"

The family began making plans. At fifteen, Leon Jr. was getting pretty old for this type of birthday party, but he agreed to suit up in a clown outfit and entertain the kids with a few magic tricks that he'd learned. The now ten-year-old triplets were delighted to help David make invitations and deliver them. They had plenty of ideas for decorations, too, and did most of the work filling the yard with balloons and streamers while their dad hung a piñata from the old oak tree. Ellie outdid herself by making her most elaborate cake ever. The entire family was excited about the party, but no one's expectations were higher than David's.

When the parents of three of the neighborhood children called on the morning of the party with excuses for why their children couldn't attend, everyone's excitement began to wane. The atmosphere improved, however, when the rest of the children began to arrive, including a seven-year-old boy whose family had just moved into the neighborhood.

"Kids, this is Tommy Rantz," Ellie introduced the newcomer to everyone while shooing him into the yard.

"He-Hellllo, Ta-Te-Tommy," David said.

"My name is just Tommy, not Ta-Te-Tommy."

"I kn-know. I'mmmmm Da-Deh-Daaaavid."

Tommy grinned. "Well, Da-Da-David, does anyone ever call you Davy? In fact, does anyone call you Da-Da-Davy the ba-ba-baby? I think that's what I'm going to call you."

# WHAT IS THE DIFFERENCE BETWEEN SPEECH IMPAIRMENT AND LANGUAGE IMPAIRMENT?

People with speech impairments have difficulty with one or more of the following:

- making sounds necessary to produce speech
- making those sounds with the speed and dexterity necessary to carry on conversations
- problems with voice quality

Individuals with language impairment can articulate speech sounds properly yet have a difficult time understanding or using language. For example, they may have problems with one or more of the following:

- They may be easily distracted and unable to follow directions correctly or concentrate on one task for any length of time.
- They may not understand language that is spoken to them. For example, a child may not understand jokes, directions that are given, or questions that are asked.
- The child may have experienced developmental delays in learning how to speak.
- Memory problems may be evident, such as an inability to recall even simple words or people's names, etc.
- The child may have a difficult time expressing herself and use incorrect words when doing so.
- The person may use sentences that are consistently simple and uncomplicated.
- Simple grammatical errors are common, including use of incorrect verbs and pronouns.

*Learning to speak is an important part of learning to interact with others.*

*Imagine if a child could not whisper a secret into his mother's ear! Speech is an important part of growing up, and when speech and language are impaired, the child will suffer emotionally as well.*

*Speech and language impairments affect people of all ages, from all economic and ethnic groups.*

## HOW MANY PEOPLE HAVE A SPEECH OR LANGUAGE IMPAIRMENT?

Estimates of the number of people with speech or language impairments range from one in ten to one in twenty. Speech impairments and language impairments affect individuals of all ages and in all economic and ethnic groups.

## CAUSES OF LANGUAGE IMPAIRMENT

Language impairment can be caused by a number of things, including the following:

- failure of the brain to develop normally
- head injury
- brain disease
- ***stroke***

- **genetic abnormalities**
- loss of hearing before the development of language
- mental retardation
- injury during birth
- psychiatric disorders such as **autism** and **schizophrenia**
- substance abuse during pregnancy (which can cause abnormal brain development)

## SPEECH IMPAIRMENTS

When elements of an individual's speech vary from normal to such an extent that it becomes noticeable and interferes with, rather than enhances, communication, it can usually be classified as a speech impairment. Speech impairments

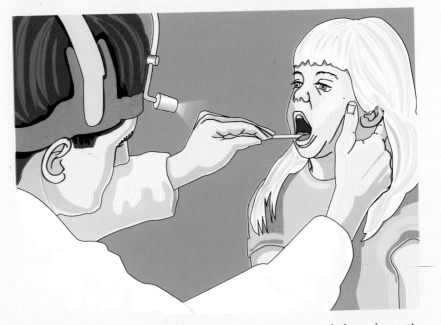

*A doctor will look for a physical cause of a speech impairment.*

*Children with speech and language impairments benefit from early intervention activities.*

often cause distress to the speaker. Speech impairments can involve:

- articulation: sounds (making the sound or using the sound in words and sentences)
- fluency: the flow of speech
- voice disorders: *pitch* (too high, too low, or uncontrolled), intensity (loudness or softness), and quality (hoarse, breathy, too nasal, not nasal enough)

According to some statistics, developmental articulation disorders occur in approximately ten percent of school age children prior to the age of eight years old. This may involve

difficulty in making speech sounds or in the rate of speech. Most children outgrow these difficulties without intervention, and speech therapy usually corrects impairments that are not outgrown.

Fluency disorders include speaking too slowly (bradylalia) and speaking too quickly (tachylalia). Stuttering is also a type of fluency disorder.

## Examples of Speech Impairments

- distortions of certain sounds
- substituting one sound for another
- omitting certain sounds
- speaking with a *lisp*
- stuttering
- *chronic* hoarseness (can be caused by swollen vocal folds)
- breathy voice (can be the result of vocal folds that do not meet properly during speech)
- hypernasality (speech that is very nasal sounding—sometimes caused by injury to the palate that results in air traveling from the mouth, through the palate, into the nasal cavity)
- hyponasality (speech that is not nasal enough—can be caused by obstructions in the nasal passages)
- consistent problems with volume or pitch
- pace of speech (either too slow or too fast)
- too frequent use of the sounds such as uh, er, and um

*These young children think they are simply playing, but they are really receiving speech therapy at a center for children with disabilities.*

*If a child's hearing is impaired, his speech will be affected as well.*

## Causes of Speech Impairment

Some children have difficulty developing speech that is clear and easily understood because of a *congenital defect*. Other times individuals may suffer an illness or injury that hampers their ability to speak normally. Perhaps the child has a problem using the muscles that are needed to produce and control various sounds. This would be an *expressive* difficulty. Maybe the child is unable to hear or to understand language that is being spoken to him and so cannot develop his own speech normally. This could be characterized as a *receptive* problem.

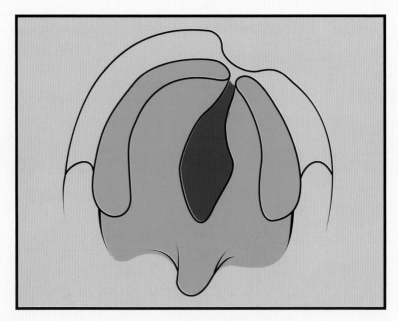

*A cleft palate.*

Here are some specific problems that can cause speech impairments:

- cleft palate (Babies born with this condition have an abnormal space in the roof of their mouth that leads to the nose. With surgery, it is possible to repair this problem.)
- cleft lip (Babies born with this condition have an abnormal upper lip. This is another example of a congenital defect that can be repaired with surgery.)
- teeth that are not aligned properly
- injury that damages parts of the body that are necessary for speech
- head injuries
- some forms of mental retardation

- some cases of cerebral palsy
- hearing impairment that takes place before the child has learned to speak
- stroke
- some psychological conditions
- various forms of developmental dyspraxia
- some illnesses such as the following:
  Parkinson's disease
  multiple sclerosis
  throat cancer (or other conditions that make it necessary to remove the larynx, which results in **esophageal speech.** It is sometimes now possible for surgeons to use other body tissues to construct a substitute for the larynx.)

*Babies begin learning language from their parents when they are very small.*

*Sometimes articulation problems may be caused by improper tooth alignment. Usually, however, there is no obvious physical cause for these problems.*

It is important to note, however, that most problems with **articulation** do not have a known cause.

## WHAT DISFLUENCIES CAN BE ENCOUNTERED WHEN LEARNING TO SPEAK?

- occasional repetitions of certain sounds
- hesitations between sounds or words
- other disruptions in the flow of speech

Most problems with fluency are minor and disappear in time as the child's speech develops. Sometimes, however, these difficulties can be more persistent and even severe.

Some problems with developing speech can be related to other health problems, such as mental retardation or

*When a very young child receives speech therapy, the parent will often accompany her.*

hearing difficulties. When a developmental speech problem is not related to another health concern, it is sometimes called a specific language difficulty. Occasionally children have both a specific language difficulty and another health difficulty.

## WHAT IS DYSPRAXIA?

Dyspraxia and apraxia are terms used to describe a situation in which children have difficulty maneuvering the tongue and mouth quickly in the manner necessary to for speech. Individuals with this impairment may omit many sounds as they speak, making it very difficult to understand them. They might also speak very slowly or in a halting manner. Children with dyspraxia have normal swallowing and sucking movements of the mouth and throat parts and do not have other problems with movement or **perception** that explain the condition. Although hearing impaired children and those who suffer from other disabilities may have dyspraxia, it is not the cause of this impairment. Only some of the children with impaired speech suffer from dyspraxia. Learning to read can be difficult for children who have been diagnosed with this condition. Dyspraxia or apraxia can also result from a brain injury.

## VOICE DISORDERS

Some people may sound hoarse when they talk; others may have a nasal quality to their speech. When these conditions do not have a simple cause such as a cold and are chronic in nature, the individual should see a doctor. A general practitioner might refer the person to an otolaryngologist (a physician who specializes in treatment of the head, neck, ears, nose, and throat) or speech pathologist for further

*A child with dyspraxia may be afraid to open her mouth for fear that people will make fun of the way she speaks.*

evaluation. The pitch, volume, and quality of the voice can all be affected by a voice disorder. Individuals with abnormal pitch sometimes speak either much higher or much lower than is usual for members of their gender. Some people have abnormal alterations in pitch while they are speaking. Voice impairment can have either physical or emotional causes.

Some diseases, such as Parkinson's disease, can affect voice quality. Parkinson's disease can make a person's voice very weak (phonasthenia). The loss of voice (phonation) is called aphonia. Laryngitis can cause temporary aphonia. Aphonia can also have psychological causes.

*Children who receive speech therapy at school will sometimes work with the therapist in small groups.*

Certain behaviors can affect voice quality, including:

- smoking
- excessive yelling
- excessive clearing of the throat
- inhaling chemicals that irritate the throat

Many people can benefit from speech therapy that is designed to correct the behaviors that have caused the voice disorder.

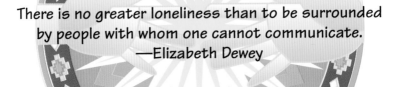

There is no greater loneliness than to be surrounded
by people with whom one cannot communicate.
—Elizabeth Dewey

# 3

# LOST IN A WORLD OF VOICE

David stood in stunned silence. He had been raised to give and receive kindness. No one had ever called attention to his speech impairment in this manner or teased him about it before. Like a deer trapped in a car's headlights, he could neither move nor respond. Tommy Rantz had taken a sledgehammer to David's birthday party.

The decorations still hung where they had been lovingly placed, yet they faded from David's view. All he could focus on was the sneering face before him. The other children also became mute as they gazed expectantly at David and Tommy.

Lily Miller broke the silence as she sprang to her brother's defense. "Hey, who do you think you are?" She gave Tommy Rantz a shove on the shoulder. "You leave my brother alone."

Theresa quickly joined in. She had become familiar with the likes of Tommy Rantz during her struggle to master the R sound. "It's very wrong of you to hurt someone's feelings like that," she said, her nose in the air. "We invited you to the party to make friends, but nobody is going to want to be your friend if you're mean."

Lily's and Theresa's raised voices caught Leon Jr.'s attention, and he quickly joined the crowd. "What's going on over here?"

"This new boy, Tommy Rantz, made fun of David," Karen explained. "Lily and Theresa were just trying to tell him that he shouldn't do that."

Other kids in the crowd began to shake their heads, affirming Karen's explanation as Leon Jr. surveyed the group before he spoke. "Okay, I don't know what you said, Tommy, or exactly what happened here. But this is my brother's birthday party, and we all want it to be fun for him and for you and the rest of the kids. I think you and David should shake hands and let's not have any more problems."

Tommy looked as though he were surprised to see that David had a brother as big as Leon Jr. That fact may have helped to propel his hand forward and contributed to his decision to leave David alone for the rest of the day. "Sure, I'm sorry *David*." Tommy said the words, but sincerity was absent from his apology.

David stared blankly at Tommy's hand for a second. For the first time in his life, he was afraid to speak. His throat felt like it was tied in a knot, and he was certain he would falter if he tried to utter even one single word. Noticing Tommy's smile grow wider, David realized Tommy knew he was afraid and that gave him pleasure. Nevertheless, David silently forced his arm up and shook Tommy's hand.

"That's better. Now let's all go over to the picnic table. The magic show is about to begin." Leon Jr. made his announcement with great fanfare in an effort to alter the mood of the party, and it seemed to work for everyone but David. The children cheered up as they followed the clown to the other end of the yard, but David was silent.

He had just learned there were people in the world who didn't like him and who would happily hurt him. He felt self-conscious, embarrassed, and fearful for the first time, and he hated it. Suddenly, he was afraid to speak; he couldn't trust his own voice. David would remember his fifth birthday for the rest of his life.

All these powerful emotions accompanied David to elementary school in the fall. He quickly developed a reputation as the shy, quiet boy. But David didn't feel shy. He felt like an energetic, inquisitive, intelligent, friendly boy trapped inside a glass jar. He could look out and see everything that was going on, but he was afraid to talk, and without speaking, he couldn't fully participate or share in the activities that were going on around him. He couldn't interact with people.

Luckily, a couple of kids from the neighborhood were in his class, but even they now treated him differently than they once had. Sometimes they wanted to play with other kids at recess, and they didn't always invite David to join them. More and more, he felt like nobody except his family really liked him or wanted to be around him. He did not enjoy school, and his feelings of isolation continued into the first grade and beyond.

By the time he got to the fourth grade, David was really feeling lonely. That's when he met Martha.

The school year was already in session when Martha's family moved into the district. Martha Phillips was a bundle of energy, and the fourth-grade classroom seemed to light up for David the moment she entered it. After introducing Martha to the class, the teacher invited her to take the empty seat in front of David.

"Hi, do you mind if I take thith theat?" Martha asked David. She was already placing her books on the desk in front of him.

David's mind was racing. He couldn't help but notice that Martha had a lisp, but that awareness was overshadowed by the fact that he had to answer her question. Deciding that the best course of action was to say as little as possible, David tried to relax. "Nnnno," he said while exhaling a deep breath.

"But thereth nowhere elth for me to go," Martha responded.

Clearly, Martha had misunderstood him; David's heart beat quickly. Now he'd have to elaborate on his earlier response in order to clarify what he meant! "Nnno, I da-dddon't mmmind."

Relief showed on Martha's face as she responded, "Oh, I thee, thankth," and sat down.

David sensed a kindred spirit in Martha, and he was intensely curious about her. His mood began lifting like a balloon filled with helium. With a slight shake of his head, he brought himself back to reality and began to concentrate on questions the teacher was asking the class.

As usual, David felt frustrated; he knew all the answers but he didn't raise his hand. He guessed that everyone thought he was stupid since he never answered a question. In fact, when the teacher did try to get him to participate by asking him a question directly, he would just look down at his desk and shrug his shoulders as if he didn't know the answer. He would rather look stupid than risk stuttering in front of the class.

David hated the fact that now Martha would also think he was stupid. Without warning, his hand suddenly shot up into the air, as though it had a mind of his own. *What have I done?* he thought when he heard the teacher call his name. *Why did I raise my hand? Now I'm going to have to answer. Okay. Okay. Breathe. Relax. Here we go.* Thoughts raced through David's mind as he began to answer the teacher. "Oooone hu-hu-hah," he began, but before he could finish the teacher interrupted him.

"Just relax, David. We're not in any rush." He was trying to calm David, but the teacher's words didn't calm him. They embarrassed him.

"Yah, *relax*, David," the boy sitting next to him whispered.

"Just spit it out already," the boy behind him quietly joined in.

For a second David was completely blocked; he couldn't say anything. *Shut up! Shut up!* "Hu-hundred ffffiffty-tttwo," he finally managed to say.

*There, I said it,* he thought. *Thank goodness it's over. I hope I never have to talk in class again. Maybe I should just give up speaking altogether.*

# LEGAL PROTECTION FOR STUDENTS WITH SPEECH AND LANGUAGE IMPAIRMENTS

Diagnosis and treatment for speech and language impairments are guaranteed to children between the ages of three and twenty-one under the Individuals with Disabilities Education Act, also referred to as IDEA.

Speech and language pathology services addressed by the law include:

- identification of children with speech or language impairments
- diagnosis and appraisal of specific speech or language impairments
- referral for medical or other professional attention necessary for the rehabilitation of speech or language impairments
- provision of speech and language services for the rehabilitation or prevention of communicative impairments
- counseling and guidance of parents, children, and teachers regarding speech and language impairments

*IDEA entitles students with a speech or language impairment to free services provided by the school district.*

# WHAT IS A SPEECH PATHOLOGIST?

Speech pathologists (also called speech-language pathologists) are professionals who possess the necessary credentials and who have been trained to evaluate, diagnose, and treat communication disorders. Speech pathologists provide therapy in order to improve the speech of individuals with impairments. They also counsel their clients and refer them to other professionals when necessary. When the client is a child, the pathologist will usually help the child's family and teachers find the best ways to help the child learn correct speech. Some pathologists are teachers and researchers. Others perform administrative functions. Pathologists work in school and hospital settings, in community speech and hearing centers, in public health departments, and in private practice.

## Speech-Language Pathologists Credentials

- master's (or doctoral) degree in speech and language
- Certificate of Clinical Competence (CCC) from the American-Speech-Language-Hearing Association
- the proper license and state certification needed for the particular location where the pathologist wishes to practice

In order to obtain a CCC, the individual must:

- possess the necessary graduate degree and have completed specific coursework.
- perform a specified number of hours in supervised and observed clinical work.
- pass the National Examination in Speech-Language Pathology.

*Some speech pathologists work with very young children.*

## Canadian Requirements

Laws in the individual provinces regulate the ability to practice as a speech-language pathologist in Canada.

The Canadian Association of Speech-Language Pathologists and Audiologists is the national organization that grants professional certification. The qualifications to obtain certification are similar to those in the United States.

### Is it necessary to be a certified speech-language pathologist in order to provide speech therapy?

No, laws in various states and provinces differ from each other. Speech therapists must meet the requirements of the state or province in which they wish to practice.

*The requirements for becoming a speech-language pathologist are similar in both Canada and the United States.*

## HOW ARE SPEECH EVALUATIONS OR ASSESSMENTS CONDUCTED?

Speech impairments cover a wide range of symptoms from difficulties with the strength of the voice, to problems articulating various sounds, to an inability to speak at all. A thorough assessment pinpoints each individual's speech problems and enables the therapist to develop a therapy program targeted to that person's needs.

The first thing that a speech pathologist or therapist must do is identify exactly what the situation is and whether or not therapy is necessary. The clinician will meet and converse with the client while observing the client's speaking ability. The clinician will listen to and evaluate the client's speech for articulation, fluency, voice, and language abnormalities. Standard tests may be conducted to assist with the diagnosis. A hearing test may also be administered to be certain that the client has normal hearing ability. When the client is a child, the child's parents may be interviewed about the child's speaking history.

## WHAT IS SPEECH THERAPY?

According to some statistics, as many as six out of every one hundred children encounter a problem with speech development, with one case out of every five hundred being severe. Speech therapy encompasses various remediation methods for teaching speech and communication skills to people with speech or language impairments. For example:

- The therapist may work directly with a child or they may work with the child's parents or teacher so that the parents and teacher can better assist the child with the development of correct speech.
- A child with a severe language disorder might be

placed in a special class with other children with similar difficulties. If the speech-language pathologist is also a certified teacher, he might teach school subjects to this group as well as aid them with speech problems. If not, a certified teacher may work with the speech-language pathologist.

- More often, a child will spend most of the day in a regular classroom and visit the speech-language pathologist at regularly scheduled times (daily or weekly). She may be the only child receiving therapy from the pathologist during these times or she may be part of a group.
- When a child is so severely disabled that he cannot attend school, a pathologist may perform speech therapy in the child's home.

*Speech therapy is often provided in rehabilitation centers for people with various disabilities.*

Many individuals with speech impairments benefit greatly from speech therapy that is designed around their specific difficulties. Therefore, the exact things that the pathologist or therapist does with the client depends on that individual's needs. In general, however, the pathologist will demonstrate correct speech and use various methods to assist the client in correcting any abnormalities and achieving correct speech.

Some people with a hearing impairment, and others who have no voice due to a physical cause, may benefit from instruction in the use of sign language. Individuals who have suffered damage to one or more body parts that are necessary for speech may need to use different types of apparatus to assist with communication.

Parents should work closely with their child's teacher(s) and therapist for **optimum** improvement in the child's speaking ability.

Friendship makes even the heaviest burden lighter.
—Willa Hubbard

# 4

# ENVYING MARTHA

Martha was different from the other kids. For one thing, even though she was nine years old, this was the first school she ever attended. As she explained to David, prior to arriving at Brookside Elementary School she had been **home schooled** by her mother.

"Wow!" David said. "Wh-wh-what wwwas th-that lllike?"

"It wath fun; thomtimeth my mom and I would go to a mutheum or to other neat platheth, but motht of the time I thudied on my own. But when I found out we were moving, I dethided I'd like to go to a real thcool and thee what it'th like."

Martha wasn't at all self-conscious about her lisp, and that put David at ease. The more he talked to Martha, the easier their conversation became. Soon David was speaking as **fluently** as he did with his family.

That's not to say that he was completely fluent, of course, but he could stutter without feeling self-conscious. He was able to get through sentences relatively quickly, without a lot of stops and **blocks**. His face was relaxed, too.

David believed that his stutter sometimes made it ugly. He could feel the stutter take a grip on his jaw and pull. Sometimes it gave his head a jerk. David hated being so out of control. At times, when he was completely blocked on a word, he would have to close his eyes hard and then open them very quickly in order to make the word come out. Other times he could get the word to come out by stomping his foot. It seemed so bizarre, and it was certainly embarrassing. He felt like the witnesses to these ***contortions*** must think he was crazy. Sometimes he even wondered if he *was* crazy. Bad stuttering memories and anticipated stuttering disasters were constant companions whenever David talked to people, but these unwanted companions faded away during his conversation with Martha.

"That sssounds rreally nneat. Do yyoou have have any ba-brothers or sssisters?" he asked.

"No, I'm an only child. How about you?"

"Aaactually, my ffamily's kkinda ffffamous because wwwe have ttriplets. Everybody kknows mmy sisters, the Mmmmiller triplets. This is their ffirst yeeear at the high sschool, and it's mmmy brother's first year in ca-ca-college.

"Oh, you have a big family," Martha commented. "That'th lucky. Do you go to the thpeech therapy? I'm going there tharting tomorrow. I've never been to it before. What'th it like?"

David was somewhat startled to discover himself talking about speech therapy. His impairment and what he went through to try to erase the problem from his life were not subjects he usually discussed outside his family. Yet he felt comfortable; he didn't mind sharing information with Martha. "Da-dddon't wworry. Mmms. Lassiter is vvvery na-nice. She'll pa-practice saying wwords with you, aand you mmmmight use sssomme machines."

All too quickly recess ended, and it was time to return to the classroom. David and Martha didn't have an opportunity to speak to each other again that day except to say good-bye before boarding different buses to return home. Thoughts of Martha and their recess conversation filled David's head with pleasant memories as the bus bounced along.

Leon Jr. was away at college now, but David told the triplets and his parents everything he knew about Martha over dinner—that she now sat in front of him in class, about her lisp, that she had been home schooled, how she was starting speech therapy tomorrow, that she had curly red hair, how they had talked during recess, and that she didn't have any brothers or sisters.

Karen's eyebrows arched as she glanced first at Lily and then at

Theresa. A knowing smile crossed Lily's lips, and Theresa said, "I think somebody has a *girlfriend.*"

"She's nnot mmmy ga-girrrl friend. Jeez, wha-we jjussst mmet."

"Girls, don't pick on David," their father said with a wink.

"I think it's wonderful that you have a new friend, David, and all of us understand that she's *not* your girlfriend," Ellie added while looking over at each of the triplets.

When David went to bed that evening he was actually looking forward to school. That was a first for David, who usually dreaded going to school. The more he thought about Martha Phillips, the more he liked her, and having a friend changed everything about school.

David was already seated when Martha entered the classroom the next day. "Morning, David," she said while sliding into her seat.

"Mmorning, Mmmmartha," David responded with a grin.

Martha turned in her seat to faced David and whispered, "I like the way you thay my name. It makth me feel thpecial." As soon as the words were out of her mouth she turned back to face the front of the room. David was glad she turned away, because he could feel the heat of a blush travel up his neck and onto his cheeks. Placing an elbow on the desk, he quickly put his hand on his forehead and tipped his face down to hide his embarrassment. But he felt pleased. No one had ever actually *liked* the way he spoke before, and it was especially exciting that the person who liked it was Martha.

Shortly after class began, David was called down to his regularly scheduled session with Ms. Lassiter. "David," Ms. Lassiter began as he entered the room, "Mr. Cunningham told me that you volunteered to answer a question in class yesterday! I'm really proud of you; that was a courageous thing to do." Ms. Lassiter was modeling slow speech as she continued to talk. "I want you to know that I've told Mr. Cunningham that you know all about relaxing and taking your time. I did that so he won't feel the need to remind you of those things the next time you speak in class. I hope that will be very soon, David. Now, let's practice some of the things that we were working on at the end of last week. I know you practiced tensing and relaxing words with your parents over the weekend. Let's do some more practicing now. Each time you feel tension in your throat or mouth, I'd like you to make a fist. Then open your fist gradually as you're able to release the tension and complete the word."

When his session ended, Ms. Lassiter asked David to return to his classroom and send Martha for her therapy session. Martha looked a little nervous when David gave her the message. Her heals clicked loudly as she crossed the classroom and walked down the hall.

One of the first things Ms. Lassiter did was to make an audio recording of Martha reading aloud. Then she had Martha hold a small mirror and look at her lips, teeth, and tongue as she repeated several words after Ms. Lassiter. Martha thought the candy-flavored tongue depressors that Ms. Lassiter had were interesting. She was allowed to select a flavor and use it to hold her tongue down while practicing sounds.

No one had ever pointed out Martha's speaking error to her before or explained exactly what she was doing wrong. Now that she was paying close attention to Ms. Lassiter's pronunciation and looking at herself carefully in the mirror, she could plainly see that she was placing her tongue up against her teeth rather than holding it down for all of the S sounds. Martha felt very capable of correcting her speech and was pleased with the session . . . until Ms. Lassiter played the tape back to her.

Martha reentered the classroom with her eyes cast downward and her shoulders slumped. She did not look up at David as she took her seat, but David was observant and could tell that she had been crying. *What in the world happened in Ms. Lassiter's office?* he wondered. *What could be so bad that it made Martha cry?*

"Mmmartha," he called as soon as they were outdoors. They walked together to a quiet spot at the edge of the playground. "Wha-what hhhappened?"

"Oh, David," Martha began sadly. "I'm okay now. I wath jutht upthet when Mth. Lathiter recorded my voithe and then played it back for me. I never knew I thounded tho terrible."

"I dddon't tha-think you sound ba-bad," David said encouragingly.

"Thank you," Martha responded. "Actually, she had very good newth for me. She thayth I'll be able to overcome my lithp very quickly. I think I can too. I jutht—jusssst—need to pay attention to how I work my tongue when I talk, and ssoon I'll be sspeaking correctly all the time."

Martha smiled proudly, but a strange and unwelcome feeling descended upon David. He realized he was jealous of Martha because she was going to rid herself of her speech impairment soon, while stuttering felt like a permanent fixture of his being.

As hard as he tried, he just couldn't conquer this curse. It felt like a noose had been placed around his neck, and sometimes it was pulled so tight that he could hardly breathe. Yet Martha could begin correcting her S sounds after only one therapy session!

A hand grasped his shoulder and spun him around. His heart sank as his surprised gaze landed on Tommy Rantz.

"Well, well," Tommy began. "What have we here? It looks like Da-Da-Davy the ba-ba-baby has a fa-fa-friend." Tommy was now in the sixth grade, which meant it was his last year at Brookside

Elementary. David couldn't wait for his enemy to move on to the junior high school. These encounters with Tommy and the small group of boys who followed him around were not frequent, but they were always unpleasant.

"Sha-shi-shut up," David responded.

"Oh, here's the thing—I don't want to shu-shu-shut up Da-Da-Davy. Do you think you can ma-ma-make me?"

Tommy had been pushing David to the limits of his patience for the past four years, and David had been putting up with it. He wasn't really afraid of Tommy; he just didn't want to fight anybody. But David's tolerance was nearing the breaking point. Now he was angry!

*How dare you treat me like this you slimy worm,* he thought. *I've never done anything to you but invite you to my birthday party, and then you ruined it, you disgusting slime bag. You think you're so hot just because you can mock me in front of Martha? Maybe this should be the day! Maybe this should be the day that you learn to leave me alone.*

David's fingers curled into his palms as his hands became fists.

# EQUIPMENT USED TO IMPROVE SPEECH OR TO AID IN COMMUNICATION

Speech therapists make use of some very simple but useful equipment when conducting therapy, including the following:

- mirrors (so the client can watch herself make a sound and compare the movements of her mouth, teeth, and tongue to that of the therapist)
- flavored tongue depressors (which can be used by a child or the therapist to hold the tongue down when making various sounds)
- whistles and kazoos (used to strengthen oral motor ability)

*Talking while looking in a mirror may help a child with a speech impairment learn to speak more clearly.*

Speech-language pathologists and speech therapists sometimes have their clients use more advanced devices to aid their speech therapy. Examples include the following:

- Califone machines are similar to tape recorders. The client makes a recording of her voice on a card, which she then slides through the machine in order to listen to the recording.
- Delayed auditory feedback (DAF) machines are used to help clients hear themselves better.
- Auditory trainers are sometimes used with hearing impaired individuals in order to mask extraneous noise in a classroom. These devices can be used with or without hearing aids.

While it is not necessary for most individuals with speech impairments to use technological devices for routine communication, some people with severe difficulties do

*Speech therapists sometimes use flavored tongue depressors to help students make sounds correctly.*

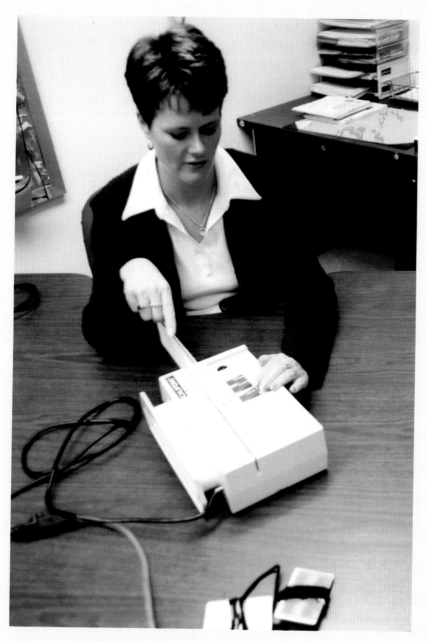

*A speech therapist uses a Califone machine.*

make use of **assistive** technology. This is sometimes called **augmentative** communication. Some of this technology is very expensive or requires skilled instruction for use. Before purchasing an assistive device, the individual should consult his speech-language pathologist. Types of available devices include the following:

- Some devices have been developed to aid people who stutter assist them by providing improved "hearing" of their own body and vocalizations that are necessary to produce fluent speech. Some of these devices resemble hearing aids.
- A system is available that claims to help individuals who stutter achieve greater fluency when using the telephone. This device plugs into the telephone and provides auditory feedback in both ears.

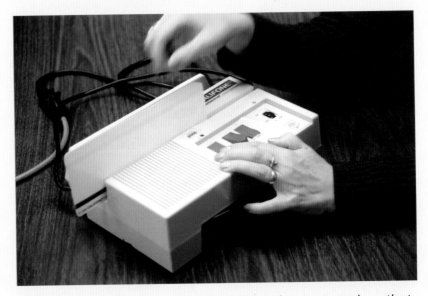

*Califone machines record the student's voice on a card, so that he can hear how his own voice sounds.*

*If an individual has a severe language or speech impairment,*
*he may use a typewriter or other keyboard to express himself.*

Individuals with severe impairments may employ the
following:

- Some people may write or type their thoughts for
  others to read.
- Individuals who have had their larynx removed may
  use an electrolarynx to allow them to speak.
- You might encounter someone using a spelling board
  that has the alphabet plus some simple words on it.
- Other similar devices display a typed message on a
  small screen or print it out on a narrow strip of paper.
- Individuals who cannot speak may use sophisticated
  equipment such as a computerized voice synthesizer
  with an audio output.
- Paraplegics who do not have use of their arms and
  hands, and who have severe speech impairment, may
  use a mouth wand to operate a keyboard.

## WHAT CAN PEOPLE DO TO HELP INDIVIDUALS WITH SPEECH IMPAIRMENTS?

- Be alert and relax. Many students with speech difficulties may appear to be withdrawn and shy. They may not volunteer to answer questions, read aloud, or otherwise speak in class. When they do answer, they might do so using short phrases or even single words. Perhaps they appear to be struggling to find the

*A child with a speech impairment may be shy and reluctant to speak.*

answer when in fact they are struggling to speak. The same behaviors can be evident if you try to speak with them outside the classroom. They may seem reluctant to engage in conversation but actually be self-conscious and embarrassed to have you witness their speech difficulty. In addition to having difficulty speaking, some students may exhibit strange or distorted facial movements or vocal inflections when trying to speak. Don't overreact to these elements of the speech impairment or make negative judgments based on them. Don't let the speech impairment become the **focal point** of your interaction.

- Have courage. Don't be afraid to initiate a conversation with a person who has a speech impairment because of a fear that you might be uncomfortable or that you might not understand him. Make a conscious effort to release any discomfort you may be experiencing during a conversation.
- Be respectful. Treat the person in the same manner that you would treat anyone else. Don't look at someone else while she is talking.
- Have empathy. Realize that this can be agonizing for the individual.
- Be honest. Don't pretend to understand anything that is unclear to you; instead, tell the person that you are unable to understand and ask him to repeat the information. If you are still unable to understand, ask him to write down the information for you.
- Be aware. Remember that having a speech impairment has nothing to do with intelligence and that most people with speech impairments do not have a hearing loss. Do not speak any louder than usual when talking to the person.
- Be patient. Allow the time necessary for the speaker to compose her thoughts and then to speak. Realize that

*Friendship can be communicated whenever you take the time to try.*

this conversation may take a little longer than one with your other friends, and don't look at your watch or give any other signals that might rush the person you are speaking with. Avoid any temptation to complete the person's sentences for her.

- Be accepting and encouraging. Maintain eye contact with the individual and respond to him courteously and in the same way that you would to anyone else.
- Pay attention. Don't be distracted by the impairment; it is the content of the conversation that is important.
- Be flexible and open-minded. If the person you are speaking with has a severe impairment that necessitates use of assistive technology, accommodate its use willingly; think of the device as an extension of the individual. Do not ask to use or play with the device. If she is accompanied by an individual who acts as her aide, remember to still make eye contact with, and address your questions and comments to, the person with the speech impairment.
- Make accommodations. If necessary, formulate your questions so that they require only short answers or even gestures. Incorporate your understanding of what the person has said into your own responses and questions as a means of checking whether or not you have correctly understood what was said to you.
- Listen carefully and look to the future. Remember that your ability to understand your new friend is likely to improve each time you speak to her, so engage her in another conversation soon.

Success, said Churchill, means you go from failure to failure without ever giving up—and one day all those failures will add up to success.
—Paula Buckner

# 5

# SEARCHING FOR SELF

Grabbing David's right arm, Martha confronted Tommy. "I'm going to thcream until the playground attendant cometh over here, and I'm going to do it right now unleth you get out of here and leave uth alone."

"Oh, isn't that sweet. Da-Da-Davy's ga-ga-girlfriend is trying to protect him. So, you're going to thcream are you?" Now Tommy was mocking both David and Martha, but Martha was not deterred.

"I'm not kidding," she responded. "I'm going to tell exactly how you thtarted thith, and you're going to be in big trouble."

Tommy looked uncomfortable for a moment, and then he shrugged. "The two of you aren't worth my trouble." He turned away just as recess ended.

"What a jerk," Martha commented.

"Yyour not ka-kidding," David agreed as they walked toward the school. "You knnnow what, Mmartha? I'mm really glllad sspeech therapy is ggoing to be so ffast and eeeasy for you."

Martha began making a conscious effort to overcome her lisp each time she spoke. One day near the end of her first year at Brookside Elementary, the speech therapist congratulated her and announced that she no longer needed speech therapy. Meanwhile, David's progress was much slower as he continued to struggle with his speech impairment.

The friendship between David and Martha continued to grow. It was wonderful for David to have someone he could talk with so easily. Martha was always respectful; she never interrupted or tried to rush David. She didn't become impatient and finish his sentences for him.

During the fourth and fifth grades they had countless conversations, but during the last half of sixth grade, the final year of elementary school, Martha kept a secret from David. David could tell something was wrong because Martha was not her usual self. He was genuinely concerned, and he finally asked her about it. "Just th-think, Mmartha, only two more weeks until summer vacccation! You da-don't seem hhapppy, though. What's wrong?"

"You're right, David; I'm sad because my dad has been transferred. As soon as school ends, we're moving to his new job. Oh, David, I won't be going to junior high school with you next year." Martha sniffed back tears.

David's heart sank. He opened his mouth to say something to console Martha, but nothing came out. It was not because his speech was blocked due to stuttering; it was because he felt empty inside, and he couldn't think of a thing to say. He and Martha had become so close; they did everything together. He thought about the afternoon he and Martha spent down by the East River shouting parts of the Gettysburg Address into a large culvert and listening to their voices echo back to them. What a great way to memorize Lincoln's words and complete a homework assignment! He remembered the two of them taking turns reading the latest Harry Potter book aloud to practice their speaking skills.

They even had their own secret code words. David remembered the Saturday afternoon when they each ordered banana splits at Smithy's Sweet Shop. Martha didn't like bananas, so she asked Smithy if he'd add her bananas to David's split because she knew he loved them. Since David didn't like whipped cream all that much, he then asked Smithy to put his whipped cream on Martha's split.

They had both laughed with Smithy about their unique banana splits. After that "bananas and cream" became their secret signal. When they thought something was funny, they'd whisper "bananas and cream" to each other or write it down in a note.

Most important, Martha had become one of David's strongest allies in his "battle of the stuttering bulge." That's what they called his effort to become as fluent as possible ever since they read about the World War II Battle of the Bulge in their history books. David just couldn't imagine what his life would be like without Martha in it. She was so much a part of everything he did now that he didn't think he even knew who he was without her.

"Don't be sad, David," Martha pleaded. "I'm already sad enough for both of us."

There was no more time to talk since recess ended, and the sixth-graders were to proceed directly to an assembly. Assemblies were rare at Brookside Elementary, so the few that were scheduled were exciting events to the students. The subject of this one was antismoking. David was happy to go to the assembly; he hoped it would take his mind off Martha's news.

This particular performance involved an individual who had contracted cancer of the throat. It left a huge impression on both David and Martha, because as a result of the disease, the speaker's larynx had been removed. Now he placed an artificial larynx against his throat in order to speak, and this gave his voice a mechanical sound.

"I don't think I would ever have been tempted to smoke anyway," Martha shared with David after the assembly, "but now I definitely know that I will never touch a cigarette."

"I'm wwith you," David agreed, "and do you know wwhat else? I'm ddone feeling sorry for myself. I mmay stutter sometimes, bbut at lleast I have a vvoice."

David's fluency had improved over the years, but sometimes he wondered if he would ever speak normally. Whenever he expressed doubts to Martha, she would tell him about some famous person who had overcome stuttering.

"Martha, do you think our pparents would let us go to the mmovies on Saturday, since we dddon't have much ttime left before you move away?"

"Let's ask them. I'll call you tonight after I talk to my mom."

"Ccall me? I ddon't know, Martha. I'm nnot very ggood on the phone." Actually, David was afraid to talk on the phone. In fact, he had only made one telephone call in his life, and he avoided answering the telephone whenever possible. David had discovered that people are even more impatient than usual when they use the phone. They talk fast, and they expect quick responses. When they don't get them, they start repeating their questions; if they still don't get an answer, they ask if there is something wrong; after that, they start to accuse the person on the other end of the line of having made a crank phone call. All of this made David nervous, and when he became nervous, he stuttered more; sometimes he become blocked and couldn't get the words out at all. *What kind of a person is* afraid *to use the telephone?* he wondered. *I'm practically a teenager, and I can't even make a telephone call. I've got to get over this.* His thoughts led him to suddenly make a counter offer. "Nno, Mmartha, that's okkay, *I'll call you* after I ttalk to my pparents."

That evening, after Ellie and Leon agreed that David could attend a Saturday matinee with Martha, David announced that he was going to call Martha and let her know. Ellie and Leon looked at each other in surprise; they were aware of David's reluctance to use the phone, and they realized the significance of his announcement. "I'm so pleased, David," his mother said. "Do you want us to stick around while you call, or would you prefer to have privacy?"

"Pprivacy, I gguess," David muttered. "Bbut I'm not rready to ca-call call her yet."

"That's fine, David. We're not trying to rush you. If we're in your way when you decide to make the call, just let us know and we'll leave the room," his father offered.

David retreated to his bedroom because he wanted to practice the phone call before making it. He was happy that no one could see or hear him, because he knew he must look and sound like an idiot having a one-way conversation with himself. He often used a tape recorder to practice his speech, and he used it now to rehearse the sentences he intended to say to Martha.

He was sounding pretty good when a crazy idea flashed across his mind. *What if I played the recording over the phone? I could listen for Martha's hello and then flip the switch to respond.* Then he sighed. *Am I out of my mind? That's never going to work. She won't say the right thing for the recorded questions and responses, the whole thing will get screwed up, she'll find out what I'm doing, and I'll never live down the embarrassment. I've got to grow up. If I can't call Martha, how will I ever be able to call anyone? I've just got to relax and make the call.*

"Okay, I'mmm rready," he announced to Ellie and Leon after returning to the kitchen.

"Good luck, David. I'm sure it's going to go great. Remember that Martha is your best friend, and she's expecting your call," his mom reminded him before Leon grabbed her hand and pulled her from the room.

David's palms were sweaty, and his hand trembled as he reached for the phone and began to dial.

## CLASSROOM ACCOMMODATIONS
## FOR SPEECH PROBLEMS

If you have a serious speech impairment that makes you uncomfortable in classroom situations, consider discussing your condition with the class instructor. She will understand your situation better, and she may be able to make some accommodations for you. Some suggestions include the following:

- Explain your speech impairment and any concerns you have about oral presentations. (For example: Perhaps it takes you longer than the average person to speak, or you make pauses in your speech that are associated with your impairment. It will be good to alert the instructor to this so that he does not interrupt you with questions or make incorrect assumptions about your ability to complete your sentences.)
- If you are so emotionally upset by speaking that you are unable to participate in class discussions, or if you are physically unable to do so, ask if there are alternatives. (One possible alternative is to make one-on-one presentations to the instructor. Another could be to share written information with the class in lieu of oral presentations.)

*Speech impairments should not place a child in solitary confinement!*

However, don't attempt to place yourself in "solitary confinement" because of a speech impairment. Your classmates will become accustomed to your manner of speech and be better able to understand you when they have the opportunity to practice listening to you.

## WHAT IS SELECTIVE MUTISM?

People who are selectively mute choose not to talk. This condition is also called voluntary mutism. The individual may have a speech impairment that has caused them so much anxiety that they have decided it is better not to speak at all. Mutism can also result from psychological trauma rather than occurring as a conscious decision.

*Talking on the phone may be a major accomplishment for a child who stutters.*

# HANEN PROGRAM

This speech and language program was first developed in Canada twenty years ago. Through this program, parents learn methods to strengthen the speaking skills of children with speech impairments who are between eighteen months and three years of age.

Individuals participating in the program become members of a support group of parents whose children are all dealing with speech-impairment. An important tool of the program is the use of videos to help parents better understand how they interact with their child and the important improvements in speech that can be brought about by altering those interactions.

# STUTTERING
# (SOMETIMES CALLED STAMMERING)

Some disfluencies are to be expected when children are between the ages of two and eight, as language is developing. A child may repeat part of a sentence or revise the sentence as they are talking, for example. They may also pause to interject information into the sentence. These occurrences are normal and are not cause for concern.

Stuttering is more serious. It is a disruption in the rhythm and flow of speech that is manifested by one or more of the following:

- repetition of sounds and syllables, particularly at the beginning of words, or the repetition of short words (This might sound like Da-Da-Duh-Da-Dad.)
- the drawing out of some sounds (called **prolongations**) (This might sound like DDDDad.)
- disruption of a sentence while the speaker struggles to speak one of the words (called blocking)

If any of these disruptions occurs frequently or over an extended period of time, the child should be evaluated by a qualified speech therapist. Stuttering is sometimes accompanied by facial tics (lip tremors or eye blinking, for example) or other involuntary movements.

More than three million people in the United States have this impairment.

## Why Do Some People Stutter?

People have been speculating about the cause of stuttering at least since the time of the Greek philosopher Aristotle (384–322 B.C.). References to stuttering appear on tablets dating back to 2500 B.C. Researchers today (including professionals in the fields of genetics, neurology, radiology, and speech pathology) continue to unravel this mystery. PET (positron emission tomography) scans of the human brain have revealed that different areas in the brain are more active when stuttering than when speaking fluently. Stuttering appears to be tied to more activity on the right side of the brain; fluent speech involves more activity on the left side. Another important finding involves a part of the brain utilized in hearing. It is not hearing of the outside world that is involved, however, but the hearing of oneself that takes place when a person talks. This area is active in fluent speakers while they are speaking, but is not active when people who stutter are engaged in stuttering activity. While we still do not know the exact causes of this speech impairment, we do know that stuttering is not a sign of reduced intelligence. It is also not caused by a psychological disorder or emotional disturbance, although it is usually aggravated when the individual is anxious or tense.

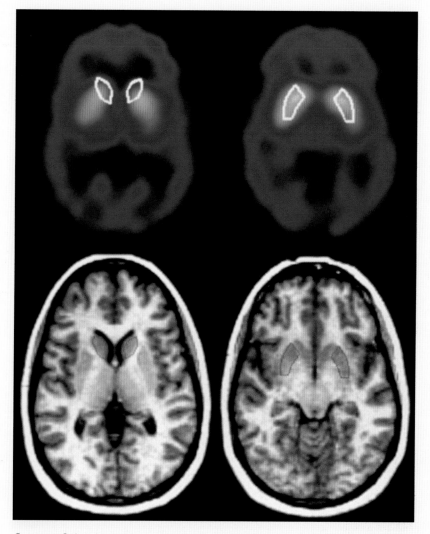

*Scans of the human brain reveal that certain parts are activated when a person stutters.*

Many people with this speech impairment do not stutter when engaged in the following situations:

- singing
- talking to a pet
- reciting memorized material with other people
- talking to a small child

Occasional discoordinations in speech are common in young children who are learning to talk. Most children who begin to stutter do so before they are five years old, and often there is some history of stuttering in the child's family. In fact, more than 50 percent of the people who stutter have a

*Support groups for the parents of children with speech impairments offer emotional support and opportunities to learn from each other.*

family member who also has this speech impairment. Children who stutter consistently, or whose stuttering becomes consistently worse, should have the condition evaluated by a speech therapist or speech pathologist. Approximately four times as many boys stutter than do girls, and boys are less likely to overcome stuttering without intervention.

Of all the discoveries [people] need to make, the most important . . .
is that of the self-forming power treasured up in themselves.
—William Ellery Channing

# 6

# A TIME FOR DISCOVERIES

David cleared his throat, and the butterflies in his stomach turned over several times while he listened to the phone ring. *Three rings, four, maybe they're out. What if I get the answering machine? What should I do? How will I sound if I leave a message? If I make a mistake on their recorder, Martha's mom and dad will hear it.*

"Hello, Phillips' residence."

"Martha, iiis th-that you?"

They talked about the movie and made plans to look in the paper to see what was playing. David thought this was all going pretty well, and he wished he could think of something else to say to Martha. "Hhave you ffffinished your homework?" he asked but then wondered if that sounded like a lame question.

"No, I still have to do the reading assignment for English. How about you?"

"I'mmm nnot done with th-that either. I'm ga-going to rrread it after we're da-done talking." *Oh no!* Did that sound like he wanted to get off of the phone?

"I think it's going to be a good story. David, I have to go. My mom is calling me to load the dishwasher."

"Th-that's okay. I hhave to go, too. See-see you tomorrow."

"Bye. Oh, David, one more thing . . ."

"Y-yeah?"

"Bananas and cream," Martha said quickly before hanging up the receiver.

*Wow! That went great.* "I mmade a phone call. I made a phone call," he shouted to his family. Leon and Ellie laughed with David as he rushed through the house and announced his accomplishment to each of the triplets.

Martha and David had a good time on Saturday, and they vowed to stuff as much fun as possible into their remaining days together. Those days were over all too soon, however, and Martha and David's close friendship was reduced to e-mail and instant messenger correspondence.

To: mmmartha@yahoo.com
From: thegreatorator@hotmail.com

Dear Martha,

You'll never guess what I'm thinking about doing. Do you remember how strange it always seemed that I could sing without stuttering? Well, I've been thinking about that a lot lately, and I'm considering joining the chorus at school this year. Do you think that's a good idea?

How are things going at your new school?

Bananas and cream,
David

To: thegreatorator@hotmail.com
From: mmmartha@yahoo.com

Dear David,

You were always a fantastic singer. The chorus will be lucky to have you. Since I sound like a frog, on the other hand, I have decided not to join chorus.

I am doing something really neat, though. I'm learning fencing! Isn't that a hoot? It's not part of the school curriculum, but they have classes after school for anybody who is interested. So tomorrow at 4:00 P.M. imagine me with my sword. That's when I'll be lunging at my opponents and chasing them across the basketball court in the gym.

Bananas and cream always,
Martha

Several states now separated David and Martha, but both of them were happy they could maintain their friendship over the Internet. David was grateful to have an understanding family.

Ellie and Leon Miller were determined to keep their son happy, but they didn't know exactly how to achieve that—especially since the family was shrinking. The Miller household had always been so active, but now that Leon Jr. was out of college and working in the city, he hardly ever came home. The triplets were seniors in high school, and they would all be going off to separate colleges soon. In less than a year, David would be the only child left at home, and his parents worried about how the three of them (Leon, Ellie, and David) would adjust to their new household. They realized that ultimately, David would have to find his own interests, so they were glad when he joined the school chorus.

David was worried about going to school without Martha, but both he and Martha decided to set several goals for themselves. One of David's goals was to get all A's in his classes. He wanted everyone to understand that having a speech impairment did not mean that he was less intelligent than anyone else. Martha had always had a terrible sense of rhythm, so she decided that her major goal would be to join the marching band.

For the next several years, David and Martha shared their hopes, dreams, accomplishments, and failures with each other almost every evening over e-mail. When they didn't have any news, they'd just wish each other "bananas and cream." David continued to develop his telephone skills through occasional calls to Martha, too.

One call that David made to Martha during his freshman year was especially challenging, because David was feeling pretty emotional when he made it. David knew that strong feelings could aggravate his stuttering, but he didn't care. He wanted to hear the surprise in Martha's voice when he told her his news.

"You'll never guess who I ttalked to in school ttoday! Ta-Tommy Rantz!"

"Tommy Rantz? You've got to be kidding! What did he say? He must be a junior. Uh-oh, he was a pretty big kid in elementary school. He's probably a big bruiser now. What did he do? Do you need me to fly over there and help you kick his butt? Tell me everything."

David laughed. "Well, I was walking down the hall, and suddenly someone slaps me on the bb-bback really hard. I was so surprised when I tt-tturned around and saw Ta-Tommy Rantz that my tteeth just about ddropped out of my mouth. There he was, ggrinning like like the Cheshire cat. 'Hello, Da-Da-Davy,' he says—only he wasn't stuttering when he said it. 'Hey Pete, meet my friend David Miller.' He was actually intttroducing me to a ffriend of his. 'So, Dave,' he says, 'are you ggoing out for freshman football? You know, I'm on the vu-varsity this year, and I highly recommend it.'"

"So, what did you say?"

"At first, I didn't know what to say. I ww-was still stunned from having him speak to me like I was a na-normal hhuuman being. Then I jjust said, 'Well, I'll give that some thought,' and wwished him g-ggood-good luck on the team."

"Wow, that's really something. So, did you mean it? Are you going to think about going out for football?"

"Yeah, actually, I am. I hadn't cu-considered it before, but now I'm going to think about it."

"Can it be that he somehow turned into a nice guy?"

"I gguess I'll find out for sure soon enough, but ya-yeah, I kinda think he has."

"Wow, I guess maybe leopards can change their spots," Martha observed.

"Oops, Martha, I've got to go. Mom's been working fulltime since Ka-Karen, Lily, and Theresa went to college. I'm supposed to have the kitchen ccleaned before she and Dad gg-get home from work."

Later, when Tommy Rantz found out that David had joined the freshman football team, he offered to give him some pointers, and David took him up on it. Sometimes David stuttered a bit during these practices, but Tommy never once teased him about it or even acted like he noticed. By his junior year in high school, David was one of the stars of the football team—largely thanks to all of the tips he got from Tommy Rantz during his freshman and sophomore years.

David no longer attended regular speech therapy sessions, but he continued to work on his own to further improve his ability to relax during speech, to begin words softly to reduce the likelihood that he would stutter on them, and to achieve his best level of fluency. He did visit the therapist from time to time to update her on his progress, to find out if ongoing research had led to more discoveries about stuttering or to the development of new devices that could assist him, and to get some pointers if he was having trouble on specific sounds or during certain speaking situations. He also discovered a tool that helped him work through the occasional disappointments and embarrassments his remaining disfluency sometimes caused—poetry.

The e-mails to Martha were how the poetry thing got started. Writing to her every day was a lot like keeping a journal. Before David knew it, he was writing about his feelings as well as just about what had happened during the day. Then one night David put his feelings down in the form of a poem. After that, the poems came quite often. Sometimes it almost felt like the poems wrote themselves, and he was just there to guide them. David wrote about the feelings he'd had in elementary school—like he was alone in a glass jar. He wrote about what it was like to feel the stuttering noose that had been placed around his neck tighten until he could barely draw a breath. He even wrote about how young Tommy Rantz had made the words in his body shake so violently and with such power that he felt the tornado they had become could lift him from the earth and make him disappear. He wrote poems about how his family helped him deal with his speech impairment and the feelings of inadequacy and inferiority it caused, comparing the strength and resilience of his parents to the old oak tree in the yard.

Martha encouraged David to submit his poetry to the school's literary publication. There, they caught the attention of a teacher who suggested David apply to the Governor's School of the Arts, a summer program for gifted high school juniors. The whole family was excited when David's acceptance to the program arrived in the mail.

# DIFFERENT TYPES AND CAUSES OF STUTTERING

## Developmental

Developmental stuttering is the type that is frequently exhibited by young children who are developing language. The child may stutter as he searches for the word that he wishes to use to express himself, for example. If developmental stuttering does not disappear within six months, speech therapy may be needed to prevent the situation from **escalating**.

## Neurogenic

Neurogenic stuttering results from an inability of the brain to precisely and consistently control the parts of the body that are needed to produce speech. This sometimes occurs as the result of a stroke or brain injury if the damage done causes a communication problem between the brain, nerves, and muscles.

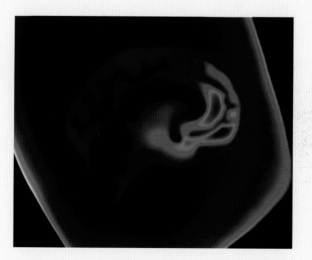

*Some speech impairments are caused by injury to the brain.*

## Psychogenic

Psychogenic stuttering was once thought to be the major cause of stuttering. People believed that stuttering was an emotional disorder or a bad habit that the individual could break if strongly motivated to do so. Now researchers realize that this only accounts for an extremely small number of cases of stuttering.

## DOES STUTTERING EVER RETURN AFTER THERAPY?

Yes, even when therapy has been very successful, some stuttering can return. It is important that the individual resist feelings of disappointment or failure and maintain confidence in her ability to control the stuttering. When necessary, she should return to therapy. It is likely that short-term therapy will alleviate the problem.

*Speech therapy is often an ongoing process.*

*Many older students will continue to receive speech therapy. The therapist may use the computer and other technology to work with this group of young people.*

## THE IMPORTANCE OF COMMUNICATION

A great deal of frustration can result when a person has difficulty communicating her needs, opinions, and desires to others. This frustration can result in behavior problems or in the person becoming sad or defensive.

Because people with speech impairments have to work through their challenge when expressing themselves, those witnessing their struggle sometimes incorrectly perceive them as being less intelligent. Sometimes children or adolescents experiencing speech difficulties set extremely high goals for themselves as they struggle to prove their intelligence and other abilities to their peers.

## FAMOUS PEOPLE WHO STUTTERED

These modern-day celebrities overcame their stuttering to become famous in their fields:

- Oscar de la Renta (fashion designer)
- James Earl Jones (actor)
- Carly Simon (singer)
- John Stossel (reporter for ABC)
- Mel Tillis (country singer)
- John Updike (author)
- Bob Love (former basketball player with the Chicago Bulls)
- Bruce Willis (actor)

Here are some historical figures who also struggled with stuttering:

- Lewis Carroll (author)
- Winston Churchill (Prime Minister of England during World War II)

- Charles Darwin (naturalist and author who developed the theory of evolution)
- Henry James (author)
- Isaac Newton (scientist who developed the theory of universal gravity and mathematician who invented differential calculus)
- W. Somerset Maugham (author)
- Marilyn Monroe (actress)
- Moses (important biblical figure of the Old Testament)
- Jimmy Stewart (actor)

*Henry James was a famous American author who struggled with stuttering.*

*Speech to Speech allows people with speech impairments to communicate on the phone.*

*Talking on the phone is a big part of most teenagers' lives.*

## SPECIAL TELEPHONE SERVICE FOR PEOPLE WITH SPEECH IMPAIRMENTS

Called Speech to Speech, this federally mandated telephone service is available free to qualified individuals in the United States, Virgin Islands, and Puerto Rico. Approximately 6,000 calls are made each year using this service. Speech to Speech offers the use of trained communication assistants. These individuals are experienced listeners of many different kinds of language and speech disorders. The service is actually a three-way telephone conversation with the communication assistant relaying information from the speech-impaired individual to the other person on the line.

Obtain information about this service from: http://www. stsnews.com/index.html

## A NEW DEVICE FOR THOSE WHO STUTTER

In 2002 a device designed to help produce fluent speech was demonstrated on the *Oprah Winfrey Show* and on *ABC News*. Joe Kalinowski, a speech therapist who struggled with stuttering while growing up, collaborated with two other inventors to produce the "Speech Easy Device," developed at East Carolina University in Greenville, North Carolina.

An individual who stutters places the small apparatus (which contains a tiny microphone, amplifier, and speaker) in one ear canal. The Speech Easy Device produces delayed voice feedback to the person using the device. According to Mr. Kalinowski, this tricks the individual's brain into thinking that another person is speaking along with him, and that can help the person speak without stuttering.

While there is no "cure" for stuttering, many people who have tried this device have reported positive results.

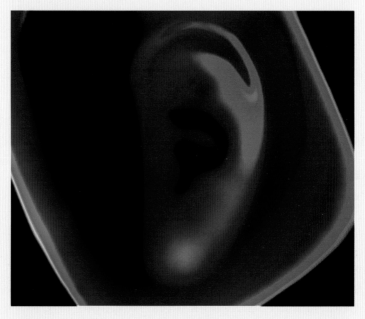

*Our ears play a role in our ability to speak correctly.*

## SPEECH IMPAIRMENTS THAT MAY BE CAUSED BY NEUROLOGICAL DISORDERS OR BRAIN DAMAGE

- speech that is slurred
- sounds and words that are indistinct and difficult to understand
- slowed pace of speech
- breath and voice control, often can be a problem after a stroke or head injury.

When areas of the brain and central nervous system that control the parts of the body that are used to make speech are damaged, resulting in those muscles being weakened, slowed down, and less flexible, **dysarthria** can result.

No effort that we make to attain something
beautiful is ever lost.
—Helen Keller

# 7

# A New Day

The two-week program was life changing for David. Students from across the state had competed for this opportunity and been accepted on the basis of their artistic talents. They were writers, painters, singers, and actors. Each of them knew how talented the others must be to have been accepted into the program, and they demonstrated their mutual admiration and respect for each other from day one. For the first time in his life, David met other kids his age who acted like they didn't even notice he had a speech impairment. They were totally focused on *what* he said rather than *how* he said it. It was wonderful for David to have his poetry admired, but it was even more memorable that, for the first time among strangers, David felt completely relaxed and free to express himself verbally.

Governor's school laid the groundwork for David's senior year. Inspired by the kids he had met over the summer, he developed an interest in acting and decided to try out for the high school's rendition of the musical *Oklahoma* in spring.

Tryouts were still a long way off, but David wanted to prepare early. As soon as possible, he obtained a copy of the dialog and music and began practicing the part he desired. Of course he kept Martha posted on all the major and minor events in his life, and she reciprocated.

To: thegreatorator@hotmail.com
From: mmmartha@yahoo.com

I'm so excited about this *Oklahoma* thing. I know you're going to get the part and that you'll be fantastic. When is the performance? By the way, how's football practice, and how's the college search going? I've applied to two colleges, but I'm thinking I need to find another. I need a "safety" school in case I don't get accepted at one of my top choices.

Bananas and cream,
Martha

To: mmmartha@yahoo.com
From: thegreatorater@hotmail.com

Martha, you were always one of the smartest kids in class. You'll probably be offered big, fat scholarships at each of the colleges you apply to.

Thanks for the vote of confidence on *Oklahoma*. The performance is April 15. I'm looking forward to the tryouts.

There's something else I wanted to tell you, and it's not good news. I just heard that Tommy Rantz was hurt in a biking accident. He's been away at college, but I guess it's pretty serious, because they're transferring him to a hospital here in town. I'll probably find out more about it tomorrow. I know he used to be the bane of my existence back at Brookside Elementary, but he sure helped me a lot with football during freshman and sophomore years. I'll let you know what I find out about him.

Bananas and cream,
David

When school announcements were read over the loudspeaker the next day, David had his answer. The principal explained that Tommy lost control of his bicycle in a near collision with a car. When Tommy swerved off of the road to avoid the car, the bicycle hit soft dirt that gave way, sending the bike down a small cliff. Tommy had suffered a serious head injury and had been moved to a hospital near home for rehabilitation.

That evening David stopped by Tommy's house to let his family know how sorry he was to hear about the accident and to ask if Tommy could have visitors. Tommy's parents were at the hospital, but his sister told David that visitors would be allowed beginning on Saturday.

David gift-wrapped a new football jersey early Saturday afternoon and set off for the hospital. Tommy was alone when David gently knocked at the open door. "Tommy," he said quietly as he entered. "How are you ddoing?"

The bed was elevated to place Tommy in a sitting position. His head was bandaged and he wore a neck brace. Big, strong Tommy suddenly looked frail. A smile crossed Tommy's lips as he slowly answered, "D-a-v-y, i-t n-i-c-e t s-e-e y-o-u."

David was shocked. Tommy wasn't stuttering, but his speech was drawn out and some of the words in his sentence were missing. "N-o-w I n-e-e-d s-p-e-e-c-h th-e-r-a-p-y. F-u-n-n-y, h-u-h?" Tommy was smiling, but David could see the tears in his eyes.

"I'm not laughing," David said. "Hey, I bbrought you a present.

Can you open it yourself, or sh-should I help you?" David pulled up a chair and sat down beside Tommy's bed.

"I o-p-e-n i-t." Tommy tore the paper. "Th-a-n-k-s!"

His visit with Tommy shook David up. That night he wrote a poem about it and sent it off to Martha, and then he went to visit Tommy again the next day. Tommy's parents explained that their son had **aphasia** as a result of the biking accident.

David continued to visit Tommy at home after he was discharged from the hospital. Sometimes they simply talked about what was going on at school or about current sports news, but other times David helped Tommy practice the things he was working on in speech therapy.

Meanwhile, tryouts were finally scheduled for *Oklahoma*. David's singing was flawless, and although he did stutter on a couple of words while reciting his lines, the crew felt it added to the character and voted unanimously to give David the part.

Football season had ended; still, David had never been busier in his life. Somehow he managed to keep his grades up while rehearsing for the play, maintaining a regular schedule of visits with Tommy, and keeping up a steady flow of correspondence with Martha. Tommy was making great strides, and on David's most recent visit Tommy shared the news that he had reenrolled in college for the fall semester.

A week before opening night, Tommy asked David if he could ride along with Mr. and Mrs. Miller to the play. "I know it's going to be great, and I'd like to see you make your acting debut," he said with almost perfect fluency.

David was nervous the night of the performance, but he did some deep-breathing exercises to calm down before going on stage. The play went beautifully, and he felt proud as the entire cast bowed to a standing ovation.

As the lights went down, David searched the crowd and located his parents and Tommy. Suddenly, he noticed the young woman standing beside them. *Martha!* David ran from the stage. Martha was still laughing and clapping as David grabbed her and scooped her up into the air.

"Is it really yyou?" he asked in astonishment. "How did you gget here?"

"Yes, it's me. My parents asked what I wanted for a graduation present, and I told them I wanted to see my best friend make his acting debut."

"I can't bbelieve it! This is incredible!"

"There's something else, David," Martha said. "I was accepted at State! I'm going to be attending the same university as you in the fall!"

## WHAT IS APHASIA?

Aphasia (difficulty in thinking of a specific word or in creating, processing, and understanding sentences) may result from a stroke or head injury when areas of the brain that are used for memory (as in the recognition of words) and organization (as in the organization of sentences) are damaged. More than a million people in the United States have this language disorder, which affects reading and writing as well as speech. As many as 80,000 people (mostly middle aged or older) acquire aphasia annually.

This condition is sometimes called dysphasia when it develops more slowly because of a brain lesion or neurodevelopmental problem. Aphasia can be broken down into several categories.

*Many older adults experience aphasia.*

After a stroke, people may need to relearn ways to use their muscles—including the muscles they use to speak.

## Broca's Aphasia

This can result from damage to the brain's frontal lobe. Individuals with this condition understand language (though some understand it better than others), but their own speech is often shortened into small words and phrases that are produced with difficulty. This is called nonfluent aphasia.

## Wernicke's Aphasia

This type of aphasia can result from damage to the *temporal lobe*. People with this condition can create speech sounds without any difficulty; in fact, they often produce very long sentences. This is called fluent aphasia. Unfortunately, these sentences are not meaningful; the individual interjects words into the sentence that do not make sense. People with this condition may also make up nonsense words. Unlike people with Broca's aphasia, these individuals have problems understanding language that is spoken to them. Sometimes people with Brooca's aphasia become frustrated because they understand what they want to say, but are unable to speak as they would like to. People with Wernicke's aphasia, however, are unaware of their speech mistakes.

## Global Aphasia

This is caused by damage to large areas of the brain that involve language. The ability to understand language or to speak is usually very limited in people with this condition.

Although aphasia is serious, recovery can be spontaneous (with speech and language abilities returning to normal in a matter of hours or days) if the stroke or injury that caused it was minor. More often, however, recovery takes longer

*Aphasia can leave a person feeling very alone, unable to communicate.*

(sometimes more than a year) and abilities do not return to normal. Speech therapy can be very helpful in achieving the fastest and most complete recovery possible.

## ADVICE FOR PEOPLE WITH SPEECH IMPAIRMENTS FROM PEOPLE WITH SPEECH IMPAIRMENTS

- Take your time, don't let yourself be rushed when speaking, concentrate on what you are saying, speak as fluently as possible, and don't feel embarrassed or panicked.
- Speak slowly and carefully, remembering the things you have learned in therapy sessions.
- Don't magnify small setbacks. Keep any disfluencies in perspective, and immediately seek another opportunity for conversation.
- Practice good speech by reading aloud.
- Remember to smile and to enjoy conversations.

## WHAT CAN INDIVIDUALS WITH SPEECH IMPAIRMENTS DO TO HELP THEMSELVES?

The suggestions below may help individuals with speech impairments, but other people may also benefit from these suggestions.

- *Develop positive feelings about yourself.* Make a list of the things that you are good at. You may be compassionate, a good listener, or very generous, for example. Read the list at least once a day. Also write the items on separate pieces of paper and tape them where you will see them often. In a dresser drawer that you open frequently, on your bathroom mirror,

*A positive attitude goes a long way toward improving communication.*

*If you have a speech impairment, you will need to let go of feelings of shame or embarrassment.*

on your desk, and on your computer screen are all good places to post them.

- *Develop reasonable expectations for yourself.* Don't expect a speech impairment to disappear overnight. Realize that therapy takes time and practice. Let go of any shame, guilt, or embarrassment you feel because of the speech impairment. Do your best to speak normally without demanding perfection.
- *Be adaptable and take some risks.* Embrace new ideas and changing situations rather than remaining a slave to the past. Avoid isolation. Be willing to try new things without fear of failure. Talk to people whenever you can; your speech may improve with practice.
- *Be spontaneous.* Start conversations. When you spend less time planning and anticipating an upcoming event, you will probably worry less and experience less doubt about yourself.
- *Develop a sense of humor.* Some situations are easier to get through if we can see the humor in them, and laughing is a healthy activity.
- *Share yourself with others.* Kindness and understanding are great attributes to extend toward classmates, but beware of the "disease to please." We all want other people to like us, but remember to be yourself without worrying that it might not be good enough for someone else.
- *Maintain good health.* A good diet, proper rest, and physical exercise—we all know they're good for us, yet we often ignore their importance. Rest and relaxation, even meditation, are as important as physical activity. Possessing physical health and spiritual health helps us to develop a positive attitude and a healthy outlook on life.
- *Don't sit around waiting for life to happen to you.* Procrastinators don't finish first. Commit yourself to

obtaining the best speech possible for you, seek therapy, and then work to make your best speech happen.

- *Set reasonable goals and then work to achieve them.* Perhaps your goal is to be able to answer the telephone without fear of not being understood by the person on the other end. Maybe your goal is to be able to volunteer to answer a question in class without worrying about what your classmates think about how you talk. Think about these goals for a moment. Neither goal is to speak perfectly. One is to give up fear and the other is to give up worry. These are achievable goals.
- *Be an independent person.* Don't compare yourself to others and then make negative judgments about

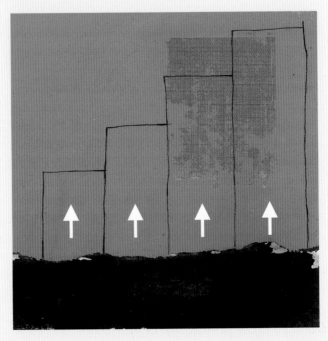

*Setting goals for yourself is a good way to keep motivated.*

yourself. Remember that each person is an individual. Each of us has strengths and weaknesses. Capitalize on your strengths rather than dwell on your weaknesses.

- *Be gentle with yourself.* Love yourself, and don't expect more of yourself than you would reasonably expect of others.

# FURTHER READING

Angelou, Maya. *I Know Why the Caged Bird Sings*. New York: Random House, 1996.

Bobrick, Benson. *Knotted Tongues: Stuttering in History and the Quest for a Cure*. New York: Simon & Schuster, 1995.

Cline, Tony, and Sylvia Baldwin. *Selective Mutism in Children*. San Diego, Calif.: Singular Publishing Group, 1994.

Cloutier-Steele, Lise G. *Living and Learning with a Child Who Stutters—From a Parent's Point of View*. Toronto, Ont.: NC Press Ltd., 1995.

Fraser, Jane, and William H. Perkins. *Do You Stutter: A Guide for Teens*, third edition. Memphis, Tenn.: Stuttering Foundation of America, 2000.

Hicks, Patricia Larkins. *Opportunities in Speech-Language Pathology Careers*. Lincolnwood, Ill.: VGM Career Horizons, 1996.

Jezer, Marty. *Stuttering: A Life Bound Up in Words*. New York: Basic Books, 1997.

Libal, Autumn. *My Name Isn't Slow: Youth with Mental Retardation*. Broomall, Pa.: Mason Crest Publishers Inc., 2004.

Libal, Autumn. *The Ocean Inside: Youth Who Are Deaf and Hard of Hearing*. Broomall, Pa.: Mason Crest Publishers Inc., 2004.

**Videos**
Prevention of Stuttering Series:
Stuttering and the Preschool Child: Help for Families ©2001
Stuttering and Your Child: A Videotape for Parents ©1994
The School-age Child Who Stutters ©1997
Do You Stutter: Straight Talk for Teens ©1996
If You Stutter: Advice for Adults ©1998

Available from the Stuttering Foundation of America
3100 Walnut Grove Road, Suite 603
P.O. Box 11749
Memphis, TN 38111-0749
(800) 992-9392
www.stutteringhelp.org

# FOR MORE INFORMATION

All Health Net.com
www.allhealthnet.com/Child+Health/Special+Needs/disAbilities/
Language-Speech+Disorders/

American Speech-Language-Hearing Association (ASHA)
www.asha.org

Apraxia-Kids
www.apraxia-kids.org

The Canadian Association for People Who Stutter (CAPS)
webcon.net/~caps/

Canadian Association of Speech-Language Pathologists and Audiologists
www.caslpa.ca

International Stuttering Association (ISA)
www.stutterisa.org/

Stuttering Foundation of America
www.stutteringhelp.org
Spanish language Web site: www.tartamudez.org

Publisher's Note:

The Web sites listed on this page were active at the time of publication. The publisher is not responsible for Web sites that have changed their address or discontinued operation since the date of publication. The publisher will review and update the Web sites upon each reprint.

# GLOSSARY

**aphasia:** A language impairment that involves difficulty thinking of a specific word or in creating, processing, and understanding sentences.

**articulation:** Vocal expression of individual speech sounds.

**assistive:** Having to do with something that helps make a particular action or behavior easier.

**augmentive:** Having to do with something that adds on to one's natural capabilities.

**autism:** A mental disorder that begins in early childhood; people with autism have difficulty interacting socially, and they may engage in repetitive behaviors and have language dysfunction.

**blocks:** Those times when a person who stutters is trying to speak but is stuck on a word and unable to make the next sounds necessary for the word to be spoken.

**chronic:** Continuing for a long duration, or recurring often.

**cognitive:** Having to do with mental process, including awareness, reasoning, and perception.

**congenital defect:** A medical problem that a baby develops before birth.

**contortions:** Twisting into strained and unnatural shapes.

**diligent:** Hardworking.

**disfluencies:** Sounds, or attempts at sound, being made by the speaker in an attempt to speak, but which instead disrupt the flow of speech.

**dysarthria:** Certain motor speech impairments that result from neurological damage.

**escalating:** Growing, increasing, becoming heightened.

**esophageal speech:** Speech of individuals who have had their larynx removed that is made using pulses of air that are ejected from the esophagus (which is the passage, or tube, used for food passing from the throat to the stomach).

**expressive:** Having to do with the ability to put one's thoughts into words.

**fluently:** To speak in a natural manner without abnormal rhythm, repetitions of sounds or words, or unnatural stops and starts.

**124**

*focal point:* Where attention is focused.

*genetic abnormalities:* Unusual conditions resulting from genetic causes.

*home schooled:* To learn school subjects under the guidance and direction of a parent or caretaker in the home rather than in a traditional school setting.

*lisp:* A speech impairment involving articulation of sounds such as S and Z.

*optimum:* The most favorable.

*perception:* A person's view or interpretation of something.

*pitch:* The highness or lowness of a sound; tonal variations in speech.

*prolongations:* Things that are made longer, as in the sounds of certain letters that are stretched out by a person as he speaks.

*receptive:* Having to do with the ability to understand language.

*schizophrenia:* A psychiatric disorder that causes a split from reality; people with schizophrenia may see and hear things that are not there or believe things that are contradicted by reality.

*speech impairment:* Difficulty speaking.

*stroke:* A medical condition that occurs when blood is not able to reach some part of the brain, resulting in the death of brain cells.

*temporal lobe:* The part of the brain that contains a sensory area associated with hearing.

*vocal folds:* Lip-like structures in the larynx.

# INDEX

# BIOGRAPHIES

Joyce Libal is a writer and artist living with her husband and assorted pets on their orchard in the mountains of northeastern Pennsylvania. When she is not writing, Joyce enjoys painting, quilting, and gardening.

Dr. Lisa Albers is a developmental behavioral pediatrician at Children's Hospital Boston and Harvard Medical School, where her responsibilities include outpatient pediatric teaching and patient care in the Developmental Medicine Center. She currently is Director of the Adoption Program, Director of Fellowships in Developmental and Behavioral Pediatrics, and collaborates in a consultation program for community health centers. She is also the school consultant for the Walker School, a residential school for children in the state foster care system.

Dr. Carolyn Bridgemohan is an instructor in pediatrics at Harvard Medical School and is a board-certified developmental behavioral pediatrician on staff in the Developmental Medicine Center at Children's Hospital, Boston. Her clinical practice includes children and youth with autism, hearing impairment, developmental language disorders, global delays, mental retardation, and attention and learning disorders. Dr. Bridgemohan is coeditor of *Bright Futures Case Studies for Primary Care Clinicians: Child Development and Behavior*, a curriculum used nationwide in pediatric residency training programs.

Cindy Croft is the State Special Needs Director in Minnesota, coordinating Project EXCEPTIONAL MN, through Concordia University. Project EXCEPTIONAL MN is a state project that supports the inclusion of children in community settings through training, on-site consultation, and professional development. She also teaches as adjunct faculty for Concordia University, St. Paul, Minnesota. She has worked in the special needs arena for the past fifteen years.

Dr. Laurie Glader is a developmental pediatrician at Children's Hospital in Boston where she directs the Cerebral Palsy Program and is a staff pediatrician with the Coordinated Care Services, a program designed to meet the needs of children with special health care needs. Dr. Glader also teaches regularly at Harvard Medical School. Her work with public agencies includes New England SERVE, an organization that builds connections between state health departments, health care organizations, community providers, and families. She is also the staff physician at the Cotting School, a school specializing in the education of children with a wide range of special health care needs.